Cotton

No other material is quite like cotton. It has many qualities which make it the best choice for countless uses. The textile industries of the world use more cotton than any other natural or man-made fibre. It is also important for many other industries and may even be made into food. The everyday fabric we take for granted is the work of a large and vital industry, employing millions of people in about eighty countries throughout the world. One part of the industry is concerned with growing cotton from seed. Much preparation and labour is needed to raise the cotton plants, harvest the fluffy raw material and turn it into a form that can be traded on the international market. The other part of the industry turns this raw cotton into the attractive and practical fabrics used for clothes and household items as well as other, often surprising, industrial products. Lewis Miles has had much experience in the textile industry and is employed by the International Institute for Cotton.

Focus on
COTTON

Lewis Miles

Wayland

Focus on Resources series

Alternative Energy
Coal
Coffee
Cotton
Dairy Produce
Fruit
Gas
Gold and Silver
Grain
Iron and Steel
Meat
Nuclear Fuel

Oil
Paper
Plastics
Rice
Rubber
Seafood
Soya
Sugar
Tea
Timber
Water
Wool

Cover *Rows of cotton harvesters in Australia.*

Frontispiece *Sorting recently picked cotton in Peru.*

First published in 1986 by
Wayland (Publishers) Ltd
61 Western Road, Hove
East Sussex BN3 1JD, England

©Copyright 1986 Wayland (Publishers) Ltd

Phototypeset by Kalligraphics Ltd, Redhill, Surrey
Printed and bound in Italy
by G. Canale & C.S.p.A., Turin

British Library Cataloguing in Publication Data

Miles, Lewis
    Focus on cotton.– (Focus on resources)
    1. Cotton – Juvenile literature
    I. Title   II. Series
    677'.21   TS 1542

    ISBN 0–85078–668–1

Contents

1. What is cotton?

Cotton is familiar to us through its huge variety of uses. Clothes, sheets, carpets and even ropes may be made of cotton. It is the most important of all the natural fibres, accounting for half of all the fibres used by the world's textile industry.

It is found as the soft, white fibres surrounding the seeds of a cotton plant. Under a microscope, a fibre of cotton looks like a twisted ribbon. Each cotton fibre is made up of a single, long plant cell. The main material that makes up the thick cell walls is called cellulose. Raw cotton is almost all cellulose, with small amounts of

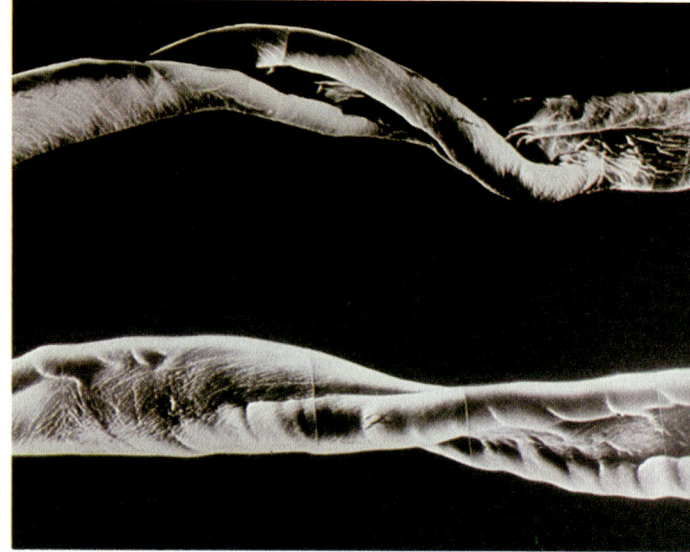

Above *Fibres of cotton under a microscope showing their twist.*

mineral salts and wax. It is the cellulose that enables cotton to absorb large amounts of water, even from the atmosphere. Indeed, cotton is stronger when wet than when it is dry.

Because of its strength, cotton may be made into fine, thin textiles as well as hard-wearing fabrics like denim. Strength is not the only property that makes cotton so valuable. Since water can penetrate to the core of the fibre to remove dirt, cotton is easy to wash and any creases are easily removed by ironing.

Below *Inspecting the cotton crop in a plantation in the USA.*

Cotton is also comfortable to wear close to the skin. It absorbs sweat so clothes do not become clammy, and for a long time it has been used for shirts, dresses, underwear and bandages. Moisture absorption is also important for textiles like towels and sheets. Cotton is comfortable, too, since small charges of static electricity do not build up readily on the clothes.

Rolls of cotton yarn with some of the finished products.

2. The world's cotton

One of the first regions of the world to produce cotton was India, where it was used as far back as 3000 BC. However, it is thought that cotton fabrics were produced in ancient Mexico as early at 5700 BC.

Today, cotton is grown in about eighty countries. For a good crop of cotton a long, sunny growing season with at least 160 frost-free

Right *A cotton doll from Peru which was made in 500 BC.*

Below *The remains of the ancient city of Mohenjodaro in Pakistan. Here 5000 year old cotton fabrics have been found.*

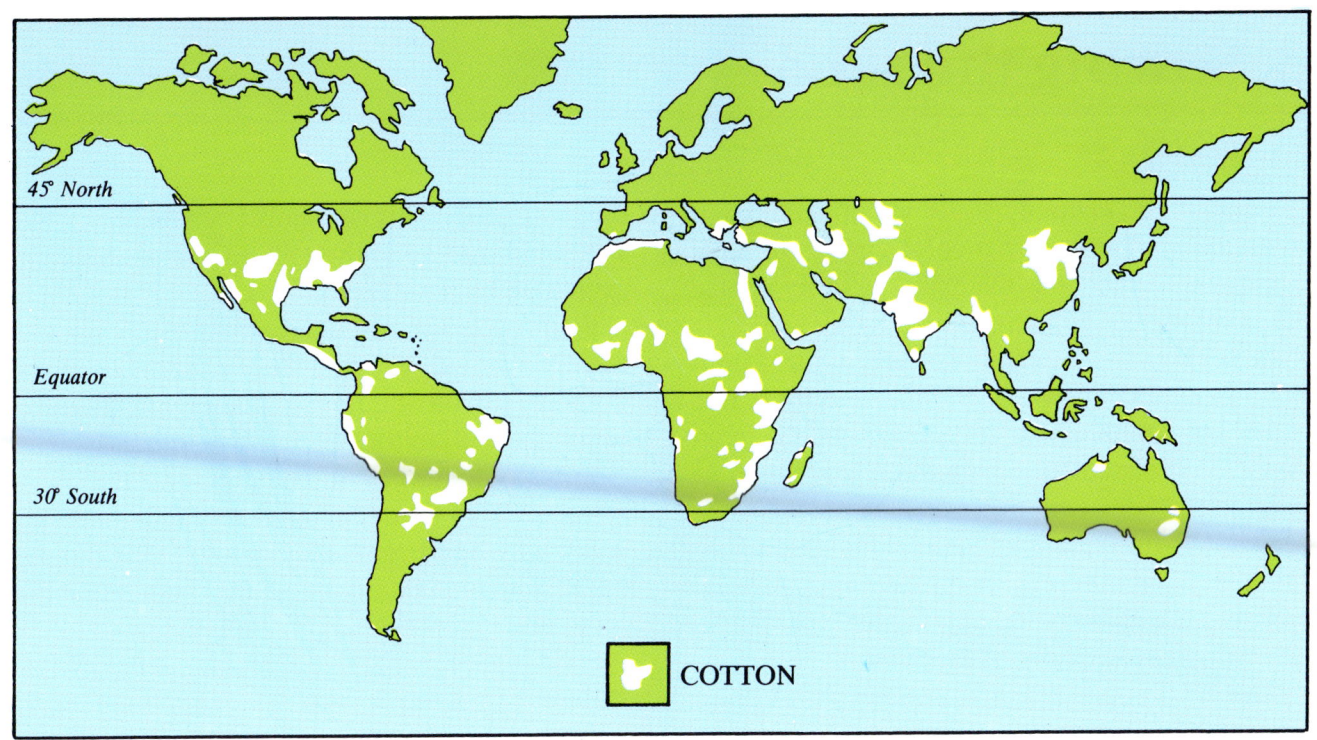

Map showing the cotton-producing countries of the world. Cotton is now the world's most important non-food crop, covering five per-cent of the planet's cultivated land area.

days and ample water are required. These conditions are found in a band that stretches around the world between latitudes 45° north and 30° south.

The largest cotton producers are China, the USA and USSR, who account for over half the world output. Other important cotton growing countries include Brazil, Mexico, Egypt, the Sudan, India, Pakistan and Turkey.

There are three main types of cotton. One type has fibres that are long and fine. This includes the Egyptian and Sea Island cottons. Another type has short, coarse fibres and is known as the Asiatic variety. With a length and coarseness in between these two are the American and African upland varieties. About 90% of all cottons grown in the world are upland varieties.

Each country grows the variety of cotton which best suits its climate, type of soils and availability of water, and is most able to resist attack by local insects and diseases.

9

3. Sowing the seed

Well-drained, crumbly soils which can keep moisture well are best for cotton growing. Soils bordering rivers like the Nile and the Mississippi are ideal.

In some places there is enough natural rainfall for a good crop, but in others extra water must be supplied by irrigation. Water from reservoirs, distant rivers or wells is allowed to run down between the rows of plants or is sprayed from overhead pipes and sprinklers. Over 60% of all cotton is grown under irrigation and it makes cotton production possible in dry climates like those of the Sudan.

The land is prepared for cotton production by destroying what is left of the previous season's crop. The remaining stalks are either shredded and ploughed in to the soil or are pulled up by hand and burned.

Planting is usually delayed until the sun has warmed the soil enough. Since cotton has a long growing season, it is best to plant early. Planting times depend on the area and the climate.

Rows of furrows are prepared and the seeds are planted in them and covered with soil. This is done by hand or by machines which can dig up to six furrows at the same time, plant the seeds and cover them.

Below *Digging a well to irrigate a nearby cotton plantation in India.*

Sowing cotton by machine in Guatemala.

4. Growing cotton

Seedlings appear about five days after the seeds are planted. Weeds compete with the seedlings for water, light and minerals and they also encourage pests and diseases. They are therefore removed by hand, by machine or through the use of chemical weed killers.

The first flower buds appear after five or six weeks. Eight to ten weeks after planting, these buds become flowers. Each flower falls after only three days leaving behind a small seed pod. This is known as the boll (rhymes with 'coal') and it contains about thirty seeds.

Below *A cluster of young cotton seedlings. To reduce the competition for light, water and food, all but two will be removed.*

Below *This boll has split open and the raw cotton is drying in the sun.*

Removing weeds by hoeing in Egypt.

At the same time as the flower opens, fibres of cotton start to grow from each of the seeds. A typical boll can contain up to 500,000 fibres of cotton. Each fibre grows to its full length in three weeks. For the following four to seven weeks each fibre gets thicker as layers of cellulose build up the cell walls.

While this is happening the boll ripens and seven to ten weeks after flowering it splits open. The raw cotton fibres burst out to dry in the sun. As they dry, they flatten into their twisted, ribbon shape.

13

5. Pests and diseases

The cotton plant is very attractive to insects. Some of them are good for the plant. But there are more than 500 species which attack cotton, damaging up to one third of all crops.

The pink bollworm is a pest responsible for the loss of a great deal of cotton and is found in most of the major cotton producing countries. Other major pests include the boll weevil, the

Below *A boll weevil feeding on a cotton flower bud.*

Above *A bollworm emerging from a boll after feeding on the contents.*

bollworm, aphids and mites.

There are many methods of controlling insects. Pests attack at different times of the year and the weather can have a great effect on their behaviour. Choosing the time of planting is important to avoid certain pests. The early burning of cotton stalks from the previous year's crop is necessary to destroy insects and their food supply. Pests may also be controlled by encouraging their natural enemies, like other insects and birds, to enter the plantations.

Spraying pesticides by machine.

Of great importance is the use of chemicals, called pesticides, to control insects. The crop may need to be sprayed many times during the growing season. This is done by hand, by tractor, or from low-flying aircraft which can spray large plantations very quickly.

Various diseases also damage and kill cotton, especially when the plant is young. One way to prevent this is to treat the seeds with chemicals before planting. There has also been success in 'breeding' varieties of cotton which are not damaged by some diseases.

6. Cotton picking

Much of the world's cotton is hand picked. This is the best method of obtaining fully grown cotton because unwanted material like leaves and the remains of the boll are left behind. Such unwanted material is called 'trash'. Hand picking is also good since the cotton that is too young to harvest can be left for a second or third 'pick'. A crop may be hand picked over a period of two months as the bolls ripen. Hand picking is most common in the Third World, where large areas of land are given over to cotton production.

Below *In the Third World it is women who do most of the cotton picking.*

Countries that are more wealthy and where the land is flat enough usually pick cotton with machines. There are two types of cotton harvesters. The picker type has revolving spindles which pull the cotton from the open bolls. It leaved behind the unopened ones which are harvested later. The stripper type uses rollers or 'teeth' to collect both open and unopened bolls and trash. The trash must be removed during later stages of cotton processing.

Chemicals are sometimes used on the cotton plants to make their leaves fall. This is known as defoliation. Mechanical harvesters work better when there are no leaves and it also reduces the amount of trash and the number of insects.

Cotton entering the picker type of harvester in the USA.

7. Ginning and baling

After the harvested cotton has been dried and much of the trash removed, the fibres are separated from their seeds. This process is called 'ginning' and is carried out by a machine called a gin.

The end of the eighteenth century saw the invention of Whitney's gin and the machines used today still work in the same way. The raw fibres are separated from the seeds by circular saws which grip the fibres and draw them through narrow slots. The seeds are too thick to pass through and the fibres are pulled away. This machine is called a saw gin.

However, saw gins can damage the long, fine type of fibre. For this type it is best to use a roller gin. This gin was invented in India centuries ago and the modern versions still use the same methods. The fibres stick to the rough surface of a roller and they pass through a gap that is too small for the seeds.

After separation, the cotton is said to be 'ginned', and it is pressed into bales. These bales are wrapped for protection and tied with steel. The seeds are not wasted, and are used to make cotton seed oil and food for cattle.

Left *Recently-picked cotton being unloaded at a 'ginnery' in Argentina. Here, the seeds will be removed from the fibres.*

Above   *A roller gin in operation. This type is better for the long, fine varieties of cotton.*

Below   *Bales of processed cotton ready for transportation to the market.*

8. Classing cotton for the market

Above *The quality of the cotton fibres is decided by the 'classers'.*

After the cotton is ginned and baled, its quality and value are decided. This 'classing' may be done by those buying the cotton or by official people from the government. The 'classer' judges the quality of the cotton from samples taken from the bales.

The value of the cotton depends on the length of its fibre, its colour, its feel and the amount of remaining trash. A good classer will have years of experience in judging a cotton sample by hand and by eye.

The textile industry also has scientific instruments to measure the quality of cotton. In some countries it is now possible to class most of the cotton harvested in one season.

Once the quality of the bale is decided, the price is set and the cotton is taken to market. The cotton is usually sold either to local mills, where it will be changed into a textile, or to a cotton merchant. A merchant sells cotton to mills that are further away, either in the country of production or abroad. The cotton is then transported to these mills by road or by ship. The current prices of cotton are published every day in the market pages of many newspapers.

Above *Bales of cotton awaiting shipment.*

Below *Merchants examining imported cotton in this nineteenth century painting.*

9. Spinning the yarn

To turn a tightly packed bale of raw cotton with its millions of tangled fibres into a fabric needs a number of special stages. The first step is to make what is called 'yarn'. The contents of several bales are fed into 'opening' machines which open out the fibres into small tufts and remove much of the remaining trash. The loose, fluffy fibres are then formed into a long sheet which is wound into a roll called a 'lap'.

The lap is fed into a further machine which untangles the cotton into single fibres and forms them into a long soft rope called a 'sliver'. Several slivers are then fed into a 'drawing' machine. This combines them into a single sliver which is finally drawn into a much finer strand of fibres called a 'roving'.

Bales of cotton being fed into opening machines.

Above *Producing yarn on a spinning frame.*

This roving is wound on to a bobbin and drawn out to its final size on a spinning frame. Here it is twisted into what is known as yarn.

For the best quality yarn, the cotton is combed before spinning. It is passed through a machine which removes short fibres in the sliver. This gives a much stronger, cleaner and smoother yarn. It is also more expensive to make since as much as one-fifth of the fibres may be removed during combing.

Right *Cotton being combed before spinning which gives the best quality yarn.*

10. Warp, weft and weaving

A woven fabric is made up of threads which run the length (called 'warp' threads) and width (called 'weft' threads) of the cloth. The simplest pattern has every warp thread passing over and then under every weft thread.

The warp threads are gathered into a sheet of parallel yarns which is passed through starch and dried by large heated cylinders. This strengthens the threads so that they are not damaged during weaving. Most yarn for the weft threads is wound on to special packages for use in weaving machines.

All weaving involves four main stages to insert each weft yarn across a sheet of warp yarns. The machine that does this is commonly called a loom. In the first stage, half of the warp threads are raised to make a gap. The weft yarn is then inserted through this gap, across the width of the cloth. The warp threads are then lowered back into the sheet of yarns. In the final stage a metal comb moves forward to position the weft thread firmly into place. The four stages are repeated, but this time the other half of the warp threads are raised to give a new gap. By repeating the whole process, a woven fabric is built up.

A 'shuttle' is often used to insert the weft thread. This moves across the width of a loom, carrying the thread with it. 'Shuttleless' looms use other methods to move the thread such as jets of air or water, and small grippers to pull the yarn.

Right *A simple woven pattern. Each thread weaves the opposite way to its neighbour.*

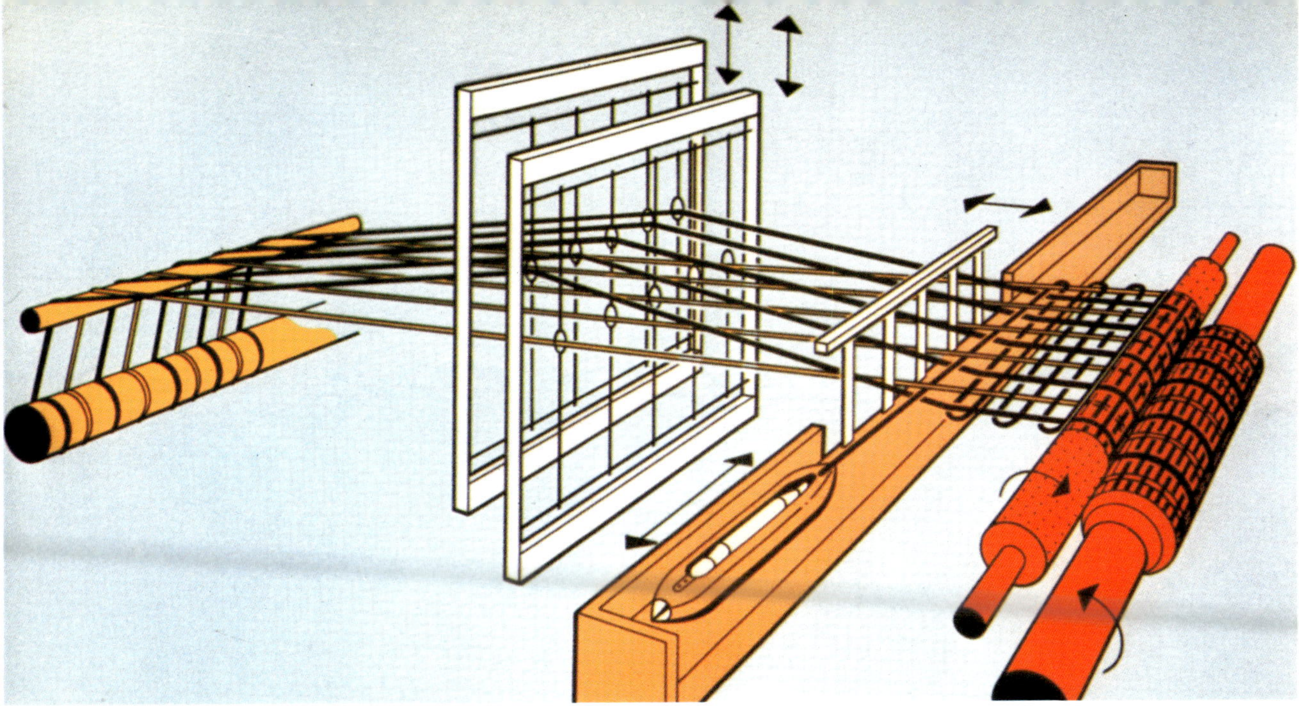

Above *This picture shows the different parts of a loom and the directions in which they move.*
Below *A loom producing a woven fabric.*

11. Knitting

A circular knitting machine where several yarns are fed in to the needles.

Knitting is another method of turning yarn into fabric. Knitted fabrics are very different from woven fabrics because the yarn is made into loops which are linked together. Each loop is called a stitch. There are two main methods of making knitted fabrics – warp knitting and weft knitting.

In warp knitting loops are formed along the length of the fabric. Many threads are guided to a number of needles and each thread is controlled by a separate needle. In weft knitting the yarn is used to make loops across the width of the fabric and each thread is delivered to every needle in turn. Warp knitted fabrics include lightweight cloths, laces and even carpets.

Below *Two types of knitted structures. On the left is a weft knitted fabric and on the right a warp knitted one.*

Above *A flat-bed knitting machine where a single yarn supply is moved backwards and forwards to make a fabric.*

Weft knitting is more important for cotton than warp knitting. Depending on machine design it is possible to produce long lengths of flat or tubular fabric from which shapes for clothes may be cut. Sweaters, gloves and underwear are a few examples. Garments that need little extra work before they are ready to wear may also be produced from a knitting machine.

Knitted fabrics are usually more 'stretchy' than woven ones. There are different types of weft knitted fabrics. Jersey fabric is the simplest and is flexible in both length and width directions. A rib knitted fabric extends more in the width direction and is often used for cuffs and waistbands.

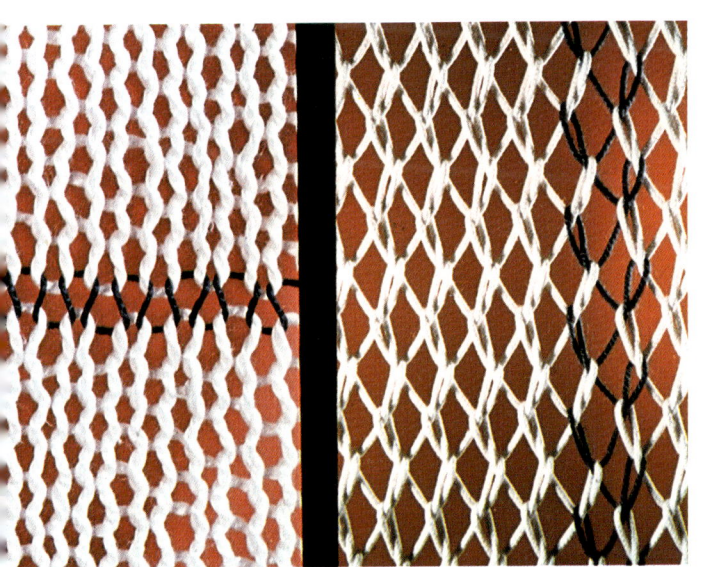

12. Dyeing and printing

Cotton fabrics leaving the loom or knitting machine usually look quite different from the goods that will be sold in the shops. Their appearance and feel needs to be improved by the use of chemicals and machines.

First, the cotton's natural waxes and the chemicals that were added to the yarn to help in the weaving or knitting are removed by boiling in alkali. This enables the fabric to absorb colour. If the fabric is to be white or dyed it will need to be bleached which removes the natural yellow colour.

Below *In this dyeing machine the fabric is passed through a trough of dye as it is repeatedly wound from one roller to another.*

Above *A cotton fabric being passed through scouring and bleaching machines.*

After drying, the fabric is white and very absorbent. It may be dyed by being passed through a dye bath. By using well-chosen dyes, colours that will not fade or come out of the fabric can be made. These are called 'fast' colours and will withstand sweat, bleach and repeated washing. The dyes used for towels need to be resistant to washing. Those for furniture like upholstery need to be 'fast' to light and to wear.

Printing can also be used to apply colour. Most cloth is printed by a method called roller printing where an engraved roller leaves a pattern on the fabric. Screen printing is a method most suitable for wide fabrics. Colour is squeezed through a patterned mesh on to the fabric which leaves behind a design.

Roller printing in action. Note the engraved roller at the bottom.

13. Finishing

After the white, dyed or printed fabrics have been dried, they undergo what is known as 'finishing'. Finishing involves using chemicals or machines to improve the feel and look of the fabric.

It is usual to apply 'easy-care' chemicals to the cotton to reduce creasing and make ironing easier. Other treatments are used to make the fabric waterproof. This involves putting a thin film of chemicals over the cotton surface which prevents water from being absorbed. Such a

Above *A close-up view of a droplet of water sitting on cotton that has been treated for water repellency.*

Below *These workers on a car production line are wearing overalls treated to make them resistant to heat and flame.*

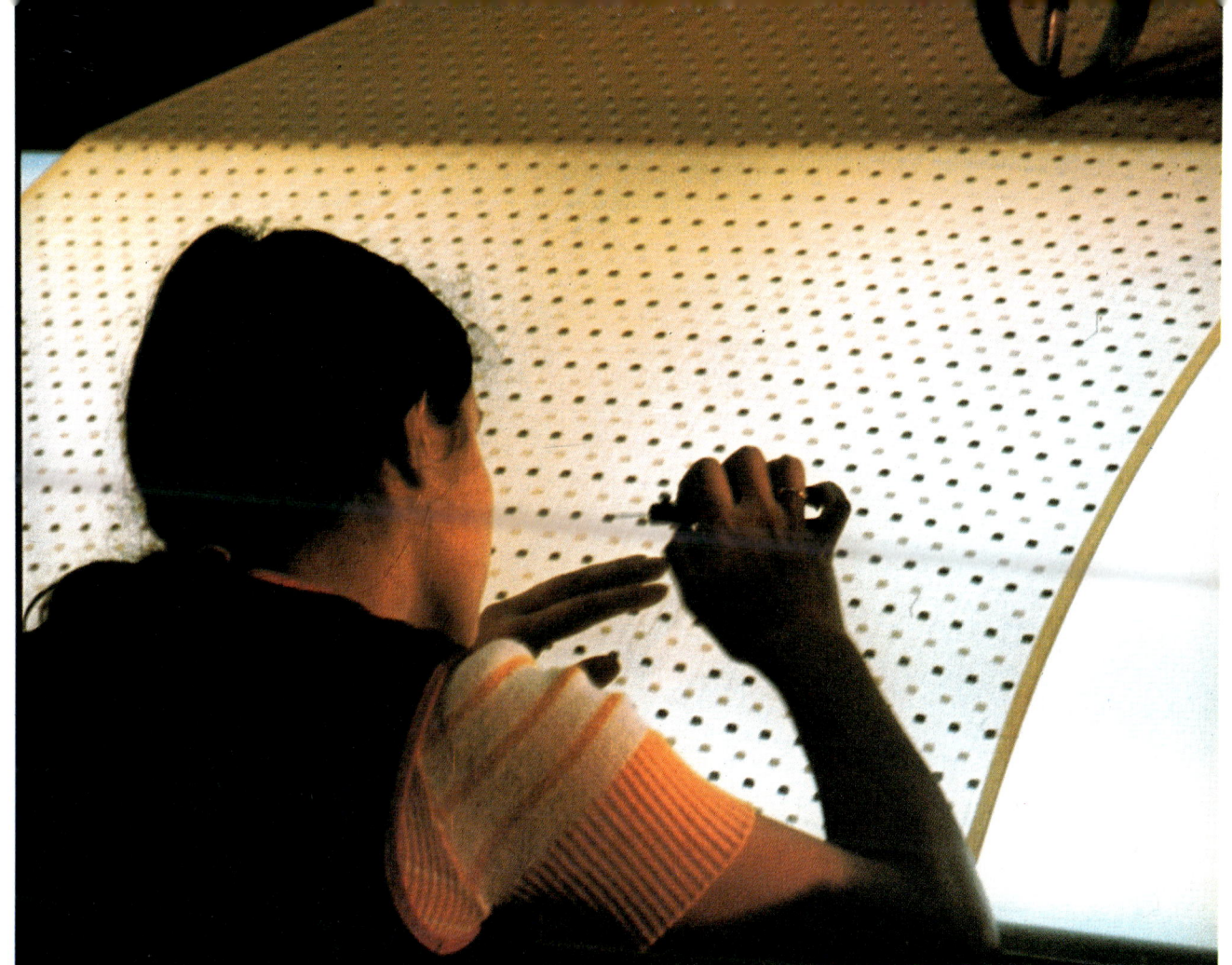

When the finishing process is complete it is essential that every fabric is checked for faults.

finish is important for tents and raincoats. Antiseptics can be applied to make the cotton goods resistant to rot and mildew. Another important finish makes the fabric resistant to heat and flame.

After fabrics have been given a chemical finish, they are often given a mechanical finish. Machines are used to control the shrinking of a fabric. Other machines stretch the fabric to the required size while it is dried. Machines can also make the finished goods look smooth or shiny. By being squeezed through rollers which have a raised pattern on them, a fabric can also be given an 'embossed' design.

14. The clothing industry

Mass production and marketing are two important developments of the twentieth century. Before 1920, most garments were individually made, either at home or by a professional

Above *Cloth for raincoats being cut by a mechanical knife called a band saw. Several pieces of cloth are cut at the same time.*

dressmaker. Production was slow and quality only as good as the skill of the seamstress or tailor. As a result, few people had many clothes. As factory-made clothing became more widespread and prices fell, it became possible for most people to own many different clothes.

The production of clothes in a factory begins at the fabric cutting table. Several layers of cloth are stretched out and paper patterns that have been carefully made by designers are arranged on them. A mechanical knife is used to cut around the patterns. The pieces of cloth are then ready for making up into the final article. This is done by many skilled people using high speed sewing machines in factories or in their homes.

Cotton is an important commodity in world trade. It is traded in the raw state, as yarn and fabric, and in the form of finished garments.

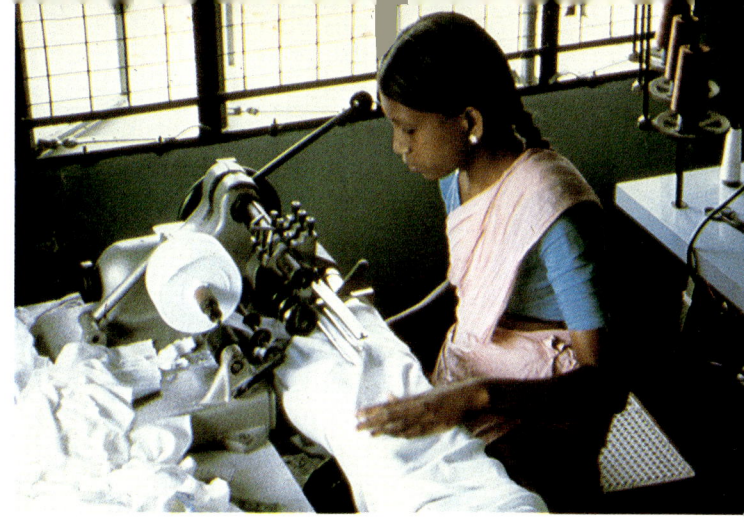

Above *Making up the finished article by using a high speed sewing machine.*

Since the Second World War there has been a shift in the production of finished textiles from countries where wages are high to places where people are paid less.

Below *In this factory in Hong Kong many of the textiles produced are made from materials imported from China and the USA. The textile industry employs 350,000 people in Hong Kong.*

15. Denim and corduroy

Over recent years it is probable that more denim fabric has been produced by the textile industry than any other single cloth. This ever-popular fabric is made of fairly coarse cotton yarns. The warp yarns are dyed a dark blue colour called indigo before weaving and the weft yarns are left undyed. Cotton dyed with indigo fades in a certain way on wearing and washing which adds to its appeal.

The creator of blue jeans made from indigo

Rows of looms producing denim cloth.

Above *Warp yarns after dyeing.*
Right *Made up denim clothing.*

denim was Levi Strauss, a German, who went to California in the 1850s. He seized the opportunity to make his fortune selling durable cotton trousers to hopeful miners during the gold rush. These hard-wearing garments became firmly established in America and their reputation moved into Europe after the Second World War. Since the late 1960s, denim jeans have become an international fashion.

Corduroy is another very popular cotton fabric. It is a woven rib fabric in which rows of weft threads have been cut by a knife along the length of the fabric in the finishing process and brushed into shape. It is used in large quantities for work and leisure wear but has many uses as a furnishing fabric.

16. Household textiles

Clothing is one of the largest uses of cotton fabrics. But household textiles also make up a large part of the market. These fabrics are not only intended for the home, but for hospitals, hotels, offices and restaurants, among others. The household textile industry produces a wide range of goods from sheets, dishcloths and towels to curtains, rugs and upholstery.

Most of the household textiles are made in the same way as those produced by the clothing industry. The cotton fabric chosen for them needs to be of a high quality and is often specially finished for its use.

Sheets and pillowcases must be strong

Warp yarns for towels in a factory in the UK.

enough to resist wear and must not shrink too much. Towels must be able to absorb water readily from wet skin or crockery. In the manufacture of towels, loops of cotton are formed which stand out from the weave. This is called a 'pile' and makes the towel softer and more absorbent.

Cotton may be combined with other fibres such as polyester. There are advantages in doing this since the product can be lighter, quicker to dry and does not crease so much. But cotton is more comfortable and can withstand high temperatures when washed – it may even be boiled.

Above *Sewing the edges on towels.*

Below *Made up sheets being folded. These sheets are made from cotton and polyester.*

17. Cotton for industry

Cotton has many other uses besides clothing and household textiles. In industry, the major natural fibre that is used is cotton. It is used for a wide range of products including ropes, tarpaulins, tents, sailcloth and typewriter ribbon.

Cotton may also be used with other materials. For example, in bicycle tyres it is used as a reinforcement for rubber.

Cotton is important in the manufacture of a range of other products. During the ginning

Cotton cellulose is the raw material for some explosives, like that used for shotgun cartridges.

process, the raw cotton is separated from its seeds. The seeds have short fuzzy hairs called linters. These linters are an important source of cellulose and are removed from the seeds by a machine which works like a gin. The longer linters have softer fibres and are used for padding and absorbent cotton. They are also used to manufacture special paper. Most paper is made from wood pulp, but paper made from cotton fibres is stronger and better for banknotes, road maps and legal documents which receive a lot of handling and folding.

Paper may also be made from the shorter linters, but their main use is in the chemical industry. Cellulose products like rayons, plastics, explosives and even sausage skins are produced from them.

Below *The paper for money and passports is made from cotton cellulose.*

Above *Cotton has been widely used as a sailcloth since the nineteenth century.*

18. Food from cotton

Above *The oil from the cotton seeds is widely used for cooking and salads.*

After the cotton linters have been removed from the seeds a machine called a huller is used. This removes the tough outer shell, called the hull, from each seed. The hulls are made into bran which is added to cattle feed, or they may be used as a fertilizer.

The remaining seeds are known as kernels. They contain an oil that is very useful and most of this oil can be extracted by a mechanical press. The remaining oil can be removed by using a solvent.

Nearly all the oil obtained from the cotton seeds is used for food. The oil is first made pure by being refined and its yellow colour is removed by bleaching. Some of the oil becomes solid when its temperature is lowered and this is used to make margarine. The remaining liquid is used as salad and cooking oil. Small amounts of the oil are used for making cosmetics, soap and paints.

After the oil has been extracted from the kernels, the remaining material is ground into what is known as 'meal'. This is high in protein and is used as food for cattle. It also makes a good fertilizer and is sold as such.

Meal contains a poisonous material called gossypol. Cattle are not affected by it, but it can be removed. In this way a flour can be made which may be used in human food to give extra protein.

Removing oil from the crushed seeds by using a solvent on the Ivory Coast.

19. Cotton is here to stay

No other fibre has the same qualities as cotton. For example, only cotton has the natural twist in its fibres that makes it so suitable for spinning. Despite the competition from man-made fibres like nylon, cotton is still the main fibre used by the textile industry.

Cotton has also encouraged the growth of a wide range of different industries and scientific research. For example, the dyeing industry has developed into the giant chemical companies. The cotton fibre is also being studied to find out how the cellulose layers build up, to gain a better understanding of how plants and trees grow.

The way in which the farmer has been working over the years to improve the land and techniques for cotton growing is best shown by what is known as 'yield'. This is the amount of cotton that may be harvested from a hectare of land. The area devoted to cotton today, around thirty-three million hectares, is still little changed from 1930, but the yield has trebled from less than 200 to 533 kilos per hectare.

The speed with which cotton can be processed has also increased. Spinning by hand produces one or two metres of yarn each minute whereas a modern spinning machine gives 250 metres per minute. Similar increases are found in knitting and weaving machines.

Right *A hand picked harvest of cotton left to dry in the sun before ginning, baling, and export.*

42

A bird's-eye view of cotton picking in Australia. This country has one of the highest yields of all the cotton-producing nations.

Facts and figures

Area of land under cotton (000 hectares)			
China	5930	Egypt	459
U.S.A.	4194	Australia	210
U.S.S.R.	3347	Sudan	368
India	8001	Greece	210
Pakistan	2023	Mexico	243
Brazil	1769	Syria	179
Turkey	620	Rest of World	5494
World total 33047			

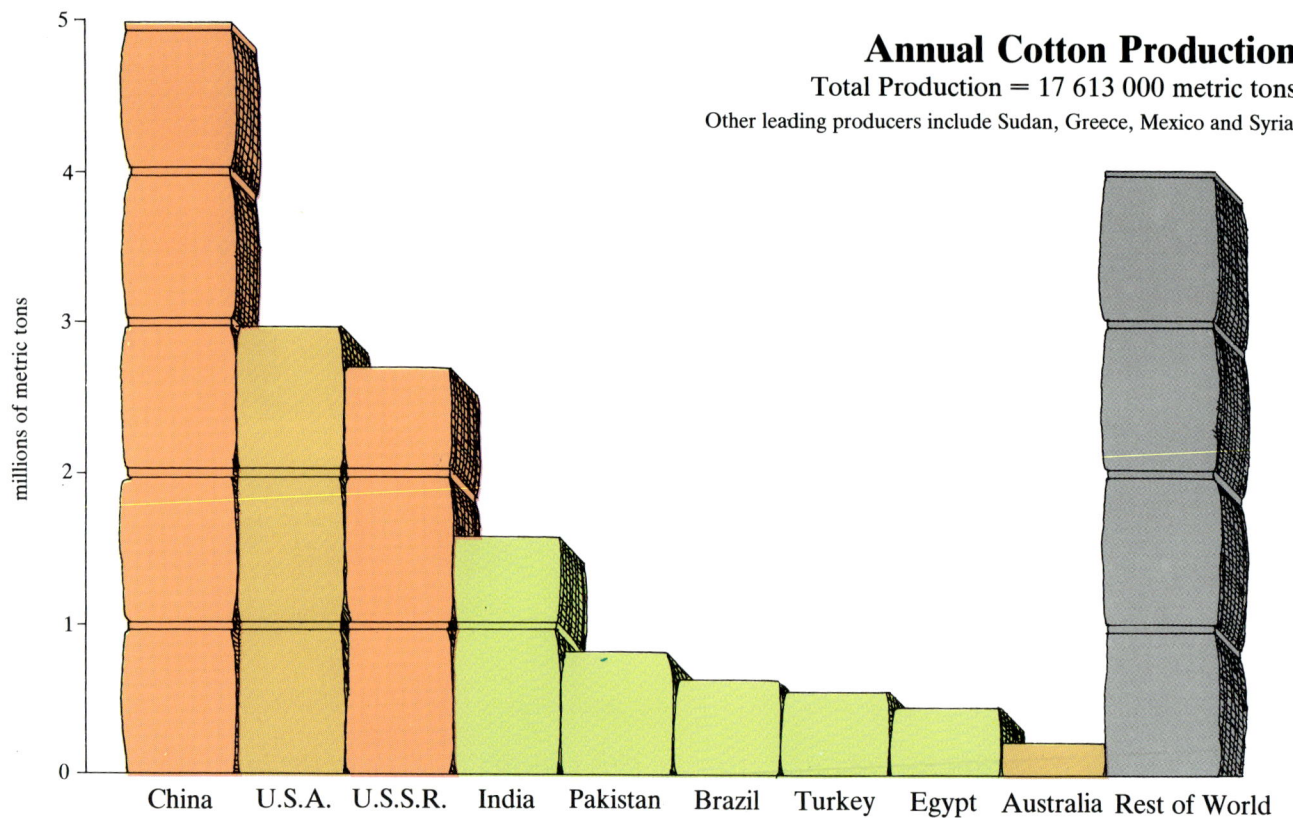

Annual Cotton Production

Total Production = 17 613 000 metric tons

Other leading producers include Sudan, Greece, Mexico and Syria.

millions of metric tons

China U.S.A. U.S.S.R. India Pakistan Brazil Turkey Egypt Australia Rest of World

44

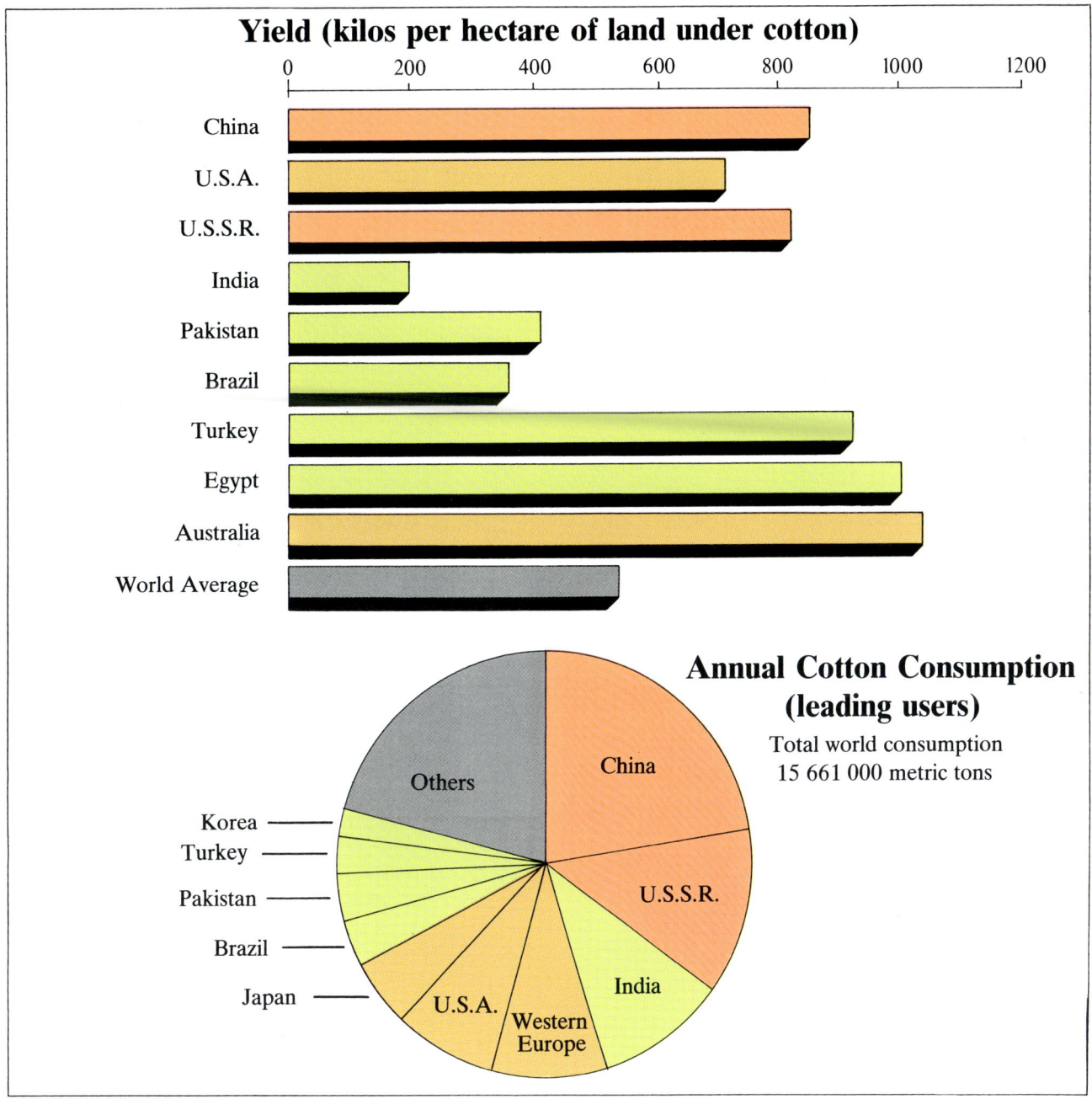

Yield (kilos per hectare of land under cotton)

China
U.S.A.
U.S.S.R.
India
Pakistan
Brazil
Turkey
Egypt
Australia
World Average

Annual Cotton Consumption (leading users)

Total world consumption
15 661 000 metric tons

China
U.S.S.R.
India
Western Europe
U.S.A.
Japan
Brazil
Pakistan
Turkey
Korea
Others

Glossary

Antiseptics Chemicals that destroy germs and fungi.

Bale A bundle of raw cotton ready for transportation to the spinner.

Bobbin Tube on which yarns or rovings are wound.

Boll The seed pod, or fruit, of the cotton plant which contains the seed and cotton fibres.

Cellulose The material that makes up the walls of plant cells.

Classing Judging the value of a sample of cotton.

Combing The best quality yarns are combed before spinning to remove short fibres and impurities.

Defoliation The removal of the leaves of a plant. Usually done with chemicals.

Dye Substance that colours or stains a fabric.

Easy-care Textile materials that are treated so that they will wear and wash well.

Fast Colour that will not come out of a fabric.

Fertilizer Substance applied to the soil to improve the quality of the growing crops.

Fibre Single strand of a material like cotton.

Finishing Process that improves the look and feel of the fabric.

Gin Machine that separates the fibres from cotton seeds.

Gossypol Poisonous substance found in cotton seeds.

Hull Tough outer shell of a cotton seed.

Indigo A blue dye used to colour denim.

Kernel Part of the seed within the hull.

Lap Roll of loose fibres.

Linter Short, fuzzy hairs attached to the cotton seeds.

Loom Machine for weaving yarn into a textile.

Man-made fibres Those produced artificially and not found in nature.

Meal High protein food for cattle made from cotton kernels.

Pesticides Chemicals sprayed on crops to destroy pests, especially insects.

Pile Yarns in a fabric that stand out from the weave.

Roving Strand of fibres that is ready for spinning.

Shuttle Device that carries the weft thread across a loom.

Solvent Liquid that can dissolve another substance. Used in extracting oil from cottonseed.

Static electricity Small amounts of electricity that build up on clothes because of friction.

Trash Remains of seeds, leaves, sand, etc. Found in bales of raw cotton.

Warp Threads that run along the length of a cloth.

Weave To form a fabric by interlacing warp and weft yarns.

Weft Threads that run across the width of a cloth.

Yarn Fine strand of twisted fibre used to make textile fabrics.

Yield Weight of cotton produced per hectare of growing land.

Sources of further information

If you want to find out more about cotton, there are several organizations which will help you:

The Australian Cotton Foundation
147 Darling Street
Balmain
NSW 2041
Australia

The International Institute for Cotton
Kingston Road
Didsbury
Manchester M20 8RD
UK

The National Cotton Council of America
1918 N. Parkway
Memphis
Tennessee 38112
USA

Books to read

ASPIN, C. *The Cotton Industry* (Shire Publications, 1981)

HARDINGHAM, M. *Illustrated Dictionary of Fabrics* (Cassell & Collier Macmillan Publishers, 1978)

HARRIS, N. *Spotlight on the Industrial Revolution* (Wayland, 1985)

MAY, R. *A Plantation Slave* (Wayland, 1986)

MILES, L. *Cotton* (Wayland, 1980)

ROBINSON, S. *Textiles* (Wayland, 1983)

Picture acknowledgements

The author and the publishers would like to thank the following for loaning illustrations for this book: Albright and Wilson Ltd. (Proban) 30 (bottom); Australian Information Service cover, 12 (right), 43; Burlington Industries 34, 35 (top); Ciba Geigy 11, 13, 16, 42; Corah plc 26; Cotton Export Corporation of Pakistan Ltd. 8 (left); Cotton Inc., Raleigh 6 (left), 17; Edward Hall Ltd. 7, 22, 39 (left); Hutchison Library frontispiece; ICI 14 (both); Richard Lohr/Ad Hoc Advertising 35 (bottom); Tony Morrison 8 (right); Nobel's Explosives Co. Ltd. 38; Sefton Photo Library 23 (top), 32, 36, 37 (top); Topham Picture Library 39 (right); Malcolm Walker 9; Wayland Picture Library 18, 19 (bottom), 21 (bottom/M.L. Perony, Musee des Beaux Arts), 33 (bottom). All other pictures were supplied by the International Institute for Cotton.

Index